Fn Bill,
a fellow student of
american history in
hopes he will like this
look at TR
With all best wishes,
Zev Gould

Theodore Roosevelt

Other Books by the Author

Reform and Regulation: American Politics from Roosevelt to Wilson

The Presidency of William McKinley

The Presidency of Theodore Roosevelt

America in the Progressive Era, 1890–1914

The Modern American Presidency

The Most Exclusive Club: A History of the Modern United States Senate

Four Hats in the Ring: The 1912 Election and the Birth of Modern American Politics

The William Howard Taft Presidency

Helen Taft: Our Musical First Lady

Theodore Roosevelt

Lewis L. Gould

OXFORD
UNIVERSITY PRESS

OXFORD
UNIVERSITY PRESS

Oxford University Press, Inc., publishes works that further
Oxford University's objective of excellence
in research, scholarship, and education.

Oxford   New York
Auckland   Cape Town   Dar es Salaam   Hong Kong   Karachi
Kuala Lumpur   Madrid   Melbourne   Mexico City   Nairobi
New Delhi   Shanghai   Taipei   Toronto

With offices in
Argentina   Austria   Brazil   Chile   Czech Republic   France   Greece
Guatemala   Hungary   Italy   Japan   Poland   Portugal   Singapore
South Korea   Switzerland   Thailand   Turkey   Ukraine   Vietnam

Published by Oxford University Press, Inc.
198 Madison Avenue, New York, NY 10016

www.oup.com

Oxford is a registered trademark of Oxford University Press

Library of Congress Cataloging-in-Publication Data
Gould, Lewis L.
Theodore Roosevelt / Lewis L. Gould.
p. cm.
Includes bibliographical references.
ISBN 978-0-19-979701-1
1. Roosevelt, Theodore, 1858–1919.
2. Presidents—United States—Biography.
3. United States—Politics and government—1909–1913.   I. Title.
E757.G685 2012   973.91'1092—dc22
[B]   2011004943

1 3 5 7 9 8 6 4 2

Printed in the United States of America
on acid-free paper

Acknowledgments

Three friends, John Morton Blum, Stacy Cordery, and Thomas K. McCraw, read early drafts of the manuscript. Their wise suggestions strengthed the prose and the analysis. The two readers for the Oxford University Press offered timely criticisms that improved the narrative. Susan Ferber was a judicious and thoughtful editor.

Contents

Preface
ix

Theodore Roosevelt
1

Notes
75

Bibliography
85

Preface

Theodore Roosevelt is enjoying a busy twenty-first century. A hundred years after he left the White House, interest in his life and times shows no signs of abating. Over the past decade, he has received the Medal of Honor from Congress for his bravery during the war with Spain in 1898. Major biographies from authors such as Edmund Morris and Kathleen Dalton have appeared.[1] Roosevelt has become a character in fiction, with the events of his life adapted for thrillers and mysteries.[2] Meanwhile, business executives can refer to a manual on Roosevelt's leadership lessons. Another author has stitched together from his writings an American history textbook.[3] Finally, the perennial debate about whether Roosevelt was a progressive or conservative rages on, with conservative authors eager to convince their adherents that Roosevelt was the dangerous architect of the welfare state.[4] Much as he glares out at the world from Mount Rushmore, Roosevelt still commands attention and engenders controversy.

Writing about his presidential administration at its close, one critic said Roosevelt had "a sure instinct for the spectacular" and had achieved "unusual and sustained popularity" in office.[5] While his reputation went into an eclipse after his death that lasted until World War II, since the mid-twentieth century Roosevelt's historical stock has shot up, and he seems to have achieved a permanent level of adulation from academics and the general public alike. Amidst a vast literature on this most charismatic of presidents, however, there is no place where a reader can go to find a brief, reliable account of what made Theodore Roosevelt so important in American history. Recent short treatments of his career derive neither from wide original research nor a deep knowledge of the historical controversies surrounding him. It seemed a good time to assess Roosevelt the man, the politician, and the president. Roosevelt, said the critic quoted above, "loved to be noticed," and what follows is one historian's exploration of why this fascinating figure continues to enthrall modern audiences.[6]

In the attempt to capture Roosevelt's significance in a short narrative, it became clear that his fame was a key to his impact on American history. From the time he entered politics in 1881 until his death in 1919 at the age of sixty, Theodore Roosevelt remained a natural subject for reporters and headline writers. Popular fascination with his career fed this sustained coverage of his life and personality. Roosevelt reveled in the spotlight and capitalized on his celebrity to advance from the New York State Assembly to the White House in two turbulent decades.

As president from 1901 to 1909, Roosevelt infused the office with his ebullient personality. His family, his controversies, his opinions on diverse subjects—all these became fodder for public discussion and debate. His popularity gave him latitude to enhance the power of his office, to pursue government regulation in domestic affairs, and to broaden the nation's role in foreign policy. The blending of entertainment and statesmanship was Theodore Roosevelt's distinctive contribution to American public life.

Leaving office in 1909 at the age of fifty, Roosevelt learned that the celebrity that had done so much for him also came with costs. Everywhere he traveled, when he went out in public, and when he faced mountains of mail and personal requests, Roosevelt tried to remain active in politics amid the demands of unrelenting fame. Running for president became his post–White House profession, and the maintenance of celebrity the key to potential success. In 1912, he succeeded in establishing an important agenda for American reform. After the onset of World War I, he embarked on a campaign to frustrate President Woodrow Wilson and bring America into the conflict on the side of Great Britain and France. This last phase, with Roosevelt almost a parody of his former self, attested to how his charisma had curdled in the concluding decade of his public life.

L. L. G.

Theodore Roosevelt

On June 18, 1910, Theodore Roosevelt returned to New York City from a year-long African hunting trip and tour of Europe. A crowd of more than 100,000 spectators welcomed him home. It was all very gratifying, but it was also time for the former president to resume a normal life. He left the crowd behind and continued on to his home at Oyster Bay, New York. He told reporters that from now on he would be a private citizen, out of public life.

The next day he took the train into Manhattan and stopped to visit Scribner's bookstore. To his surprise and dismay, his mere presence attracted a throng of spectators. As he wrote to his sister, "When I came out a short while afterward, a huge crowd had assembled and literally they would not let me pass. They wanted to carry me on their shoulders; they wanted to do utterly impossible and objectionable things; and I realized at once that this was not the friendly reception of yesterday, but that it represented a certain hysterical quality which boded ill for my future."[7]

This small episode in Roosevelt's life captures something of the special quality that Roosevelt brought to public life from his entry into politics until his death. While he was a serious thinker who pondered the future of an industrial society and the role of government, Roosevelt was also something rarer. He was the political equivalent of a movie star, with a persona distinct from his everyday labors in governing the nation and shaping its policies. The educational philosopher John Dewey observed that Roosevelt had a "double." It consisted "of the acts of the original individual reflected first in the imaginations and then in the desires and acts of other men. Just because Roosevelt's capture of the imagination of his countrymen was so complete, his public double was immense, towering."[8]

Consider what is most remembered about Theodore Roosevelt—his Rough Rider hat, his pince-nez glasses, his prominent teeth, and his bushy mustache. They combine into an iconic presence, whether on Mount Rushmore, in advertising, or on stage and screen. Few people who knew him well ever called him "Teddy," but today everyone knows "Teddy" Roosevelt—whenever a charge up Kettle Hill on the San Juan Heights in Cuba is recalled, the "bully pulpit" is invoked, or the Bull Moose presidential campaign of 1912 is mentioned. He was a man in control of his image and personality when he rounded up cattle thieves on the Dakota prairie, raced with his men toward Spanish rifles, and gave a speech in 1912 with a bullet lodged in his body after an assassination attempt. Only on rare occasions, as when he was jostled outside a bookstore, did he seem out of sync with his adoring public.

Roosevelt's life spanned the dawning age of celebrity in the late nineteenth century and the emergence of stardom with the advent of motion pictures. From his earliest moments in the arena Roosevelt achieved fame, and his activities were imbued with a sense in the public mind that whatever he did mattered. He possessed a kind of magnetism that, as one friend noted, "surrounded him as kind of nimbus, imperceptible but irresistibly drawing to him everyone who came into his presence—even those who believed they were antagonistic or inimical to him."[9] In his rise to the White House, Roosevelt managed with great deftness his fame to his political advantage. Once he succeeded William McKinley in 1901, he personalized the presidency in a manner that blended serious policy achievements and the exploitation of the popular fascination with him as a charismatic individual. Only in the last decade of his life, when he fell back on celebrity in the absence of power, did the strains and ambiguities of stardom take his life in less productive directions.

"My father, Theodore Roosevelt, was the best man I ever knew." (Theodore Roosevelt on his father, whose name he shared[10])

Theodore Roosevelt was born on October 27, 1858, at 28 East 20th Street in New York City. His father, Theodore Roosevelt Sr., a glass importer and later a prestigious Manhattan philanthropist, assured his eldest son shortly before his death in 1878 that he "was the dearest of his children to him." More important for young Theodore was the instant public recognition that came with his father's famous name and the accruing credibility that accompanied his good works for charitable causes.[11]

The elder Theodore encouraged his second child's physical development, helped him overcome childhood asthma, and offered in his own losing political struggles against New York's Republican bosses an incentive for the son's public career. Roosevelt's mother, Martha (Mittie) Bulloch Roosevelt, a native of Georgia, sympathized with the cause of the South; several of her relatives wore Confederate grey. Accordingly, Theodore Sr. hired a substitute to take his place in the Union Army and practiced good works as a civilian. The failure of his father to volunteer for combat in this national crisis haunted his son. In later potential military confrontations, Roosevelt sought out active service. "I did not intend to have to hire somebody else to do my shooting for me," he stated in 1907.[12]

Chronic illness brought out his determination to implement his father's command to "make" his body. While full vigor eluded him until early manhood, he acquired a taste for sports and outdoor activity that made him the propronent of what he called "the strenuous life." Forced to stay indoors because of his asthma, he trained himself to be an expert amateur naturalist. He assembled an array of diverse and sometimes foul-smelling small animals and birds. At thirteen he was fitted with glasses to correct his defective eyesight. Despite the limits of his poor vision, he had long been an avid consumer of books. He would, in time, emerge as one of the best read of all American presidents.

Roosevelt grew up in a loving and comfortable family. "Old money" gave his father the chance to pursue uplifting programs for newsboys and others among New York's poor. The elder Theodore built a reputation as one of the city's most dedicated benefactors. Wealth also insured that Roosevelt, his younger brother, Elliott, and his two sisters, Anna (Bamie) and Corinne, would start out in life with secure incomes from bequests of $125,000 in their father's will. Martha Bulloch Roosevelt became more detached from the world in later life, but she imparted to her son some of the allure of the Old South and the useful political gift of personal ties to Dixie. Roosevelt later claimed: "I am half Southern." As Theodore left for Harvard College in September 1876, his father called him "a boy in whom I could place perfect trust and confidence."[13]

At Harvard, Roosevelt studied hard, boxed and rowed, and edited a campus journal, the *Advocate* . As a student, he was irrepressible, peppering the faculty with questions. "Now look here, Roosevelt," said his geology professor, "let me talk, I'm running this course." His personal income of $8,000 annually exceeded that of Harvard's president, and he plunged into the life of aristocratic clubs such as the Porcellian. His father's death from cancer in early 1878 was a severe personal blow, but with youthful resilience he enjoyed a golden experience during his senior year at Harvard. He told his sister, "I stand 19th in the class, which began with 230 fellows. Only one gentleman stands ahead of me."[14]

His college years also brought him romance. In October of his junior year, he met his first wife. Alice Lee was seventeen and came from a well-to-do Boston family. She became, he wrote, "my first love, too," though there had been earlier an infatuation with a childhood friend, Edith Carow. Theodore pursued Alice through the winter and spring of 1879. "See that girl?" he said to a friend at a party. "I am going to marry her. She won't have me, but I am going to have her!" She rejected his initial proposal, but then in January 1880 she accepted. They were married on October 27, 1880, his twenty-second birthday.[15]

After graduation in the spring of 1880, Roosevelt returned to New York, studied law, invested in western cattle ranching and wrote the thorough and technical *Naval History of the War of 1812*. It was the first of many books on nature, politics, and history. But a life of leisure and scholarship did not follow. Election to the New York State Assembly during the fall of 1881 launched his career in politics. Years later Roosevelt observed, "A young man of my bringing-up and convictions could join only the Republican party, and join it I accordingly did."[16] His selection as a candidate in the Twenty-First Assembly District came about in part because local leaders, including his future ally Elihu Root, spotted him as a potential young candidate when he finished college. They cleared the way by persuading a possible rival "to retire and let us put Roosevelt in his place."[17]

Roosevelt's commitment to the Republicans began a lifelong and difficult relationship with the Grand Old Party. An admirer of the Union side in the Civil War, Roosevelt found a natural home with the party that emphasized nationalism, patriotism, and economic growth. Not interested in entrepreneurial ventures himself, he paid less attention to the close ties between the Republicans and the business community in the North. Republicans believed with an almost religious devotion in the protective tariff. High duties on foreign imports, they asserted, encouraged American industry, raised the wages of workers, and diffused benefits throughout the economy. Roosevelt never shared this reverence for the tariff, but he agreed with most of the other ways that his party asserted national power to promote economic growth.

Yet a commitment to the Republicans also imposed constraints on the ambitious and energetic politician. Even though it had only been in existence for only a quarter of a century, the party already followed a hierarchical process in which faithful service to the organization was rewarded only late in life. But Roosevelt was unwilling to wait for the accumulation of IOUs through unsung work for party leaders to accomplish his own advancement. His genius lay in grasping that fame and celebrity could enable him to leap up the political ladder. The key was to make a name for himself and remain in the public sphere, which he did with uncommon skill for the two decades after he left college.

> **"Immediately after leaving college I went to the legislature. I was the youngest man there, and I rose like a rocket."[18]**

Roosevelt first captured newspaper attention in the New York Assembly. Contrary to later legend, his family approved of his candidacy and watched with pride as he immersed himself in the new and colorful world of Republican municipal and state politics. Although he had much to learn about legislative practices, the young politician displayed a striking aptitude for his new profession. To his fellow lawmakers, he may have seemed like a Manhattan "dude" in his fancy clothes, but they responded to his sincerity and energy. His high, squeaky voice became a familiar sound in the chamber as he debated bills, offered amendments, and cultivated his public persona for the members and the watching reporters.

Service in the assembly expanded his knowledge of the world beyond his home and Harvard. Reelected in 1882 and 1883, he sponsored legislation to improve the working conditions of cigar workers, pursued a corrupt state judge, opposed the railroad magnate Jay Gould, and even did battle with Democratic governor Grover Cleveland. He blossomed in the spotlight of public attention and soon gained national attention. A Washington, D.C., newspaper in April 1884 called him "in some respects one of the most remarkable young men of his day."[19]

Two months earlier, tragedy had struck the young politician. Alice Roosevelt contracted a kidney disease during pregnancy. After her daughter was born on February 12, 1884, Alice slipped into unconsciousness. At the same time, Roosevelt's mother fell ill with typhoid fever. "There is a curse on this house!" said his brother, Elliott. "Mother is dying, and Alice is dying too." They died within hours of each other on February 14, 1884. The baby, named Alice after her mother, survived. A stricken Roosevelt published a memorial address in which he said, "And when my heart's dearest died, the light went out from my life for ever."[20] Once the formal prescribed mourning period for Alice was over, Roosevelt rarely spoke of Alice again and called his daughter by names other than her own.

In the spring of 1884, Roosevelt had to deal with the contest raging in the Republican Party over the proposed nomination of James G. Blaine, the "Plumed Knight" of

Maine, for the presidency. Supporting Blaine would have been a cautious course. The most popular Republican of his time and the champion of the protective tariff, Blaine was all but assured of garnering the party nomination. But for Roosevelt and the Republicans he knew in New York, Blaine's popularity came with a baggage of ethical lapses committed during his years as a House member and then senator. Therefore, the young legislator aligned himself with the long-shot candidacy of Senator George F. Edmunds of Vermont.

At the Republican convention, Roosevelt grabbed headlines as a leader of the anti-Blaine coalition. He rallied the Blaine opponents around his man, but in the end could not block the winner. Nonetheless, the publicity was priceless. Watching Roosevelt's performance at the convention, one Republican concluded that the young man "will not prove to be a great political manager," but in fact Roosevelt's direction of the Edmunds bloc brought him an initial taste of national publicity.[21]

Eastern Republicans of a reform bent disliked Blaine's claim to the allegiance of rank-and-file GOP members and found his financial dealings in Congress questionable. These wavering Republicans expected Roosevelt to join other party dissidents who were bolting to Grover Cleveland. Even before the nomination of Blaine, Roosevelt and a new friend, Henry Cabot Lodge of Massachusetts, had decided that they would have to support the nominee of the Republican convention. They knew, as Roosevelt said, that Blaine's selection was "demanded by the irresistible desire of the Republican party."[22]

At first, Roosevelt said he would not take any part in the national campaign, but by October he was defending Blaine and attacking Cleveland. He could not have followed another course and remained effective as a Republican. In that era of intense partisanship, bolting the ticket and voting Democratic would have ended any chance of further advancement within the GOP. What was more striking about the episode was the extent of national press coverage of the decision of a three-term member of the New York Assembly about the outcome of the election. Already, after only three years in the public eye, Theodore Roosevelt had attained an enviable amount of political notoriety.

"I do not believe there ever was any life more attractive to a vigorous young fellow than life on a cattle-ranch in those days."[23]

Out of office, Roosevelt took up cattle ranching in the Dakotas as a catharsis after the death of his wife and mother. He had first invested in the region in 1882, and a year later he put his money, which amounted to almost

20 percent of his estate, into two cattle ranches, the Maltese Cross and the Elkhorn, in the Dakota Badlands. Roosevelt's years in Dakota infused his life with even more color and drama. Cowboys in the territory remembered his orders to them: "Hasten forward quickly there." Men talked of how he floored an armed, drunken antagonist with a single blow in a Montana saloon. He shot bears, battled blizzards, and kept on reading. In April 1886 he and two friends pursued and captured, and then he alone brought to the local sheriff three thieves who had stolen a boat from his Elkhorn ranch. While doing all this, he read all of Leo Tolstoy's *Anna Karenina* in French. Stories of his exploits appeared in Eastern newspapers. To be sure that the world knew of his activities, he wrote articles for popular magazines about what he had done.[24]

By the fall of 1886, the cattle boom was ending. The hard winter of 1886–87, in which thousands of steers died and investors suffered substantial losses, depleted Roosevelt's stake. The monetary setback was large, and he had to write books and articles to support his expensive lifestyle. The gains in physical and emotional well-being and political appeal from his years in the West persisted. In 1910, he told an audience in Fargo, North Dakota, "The most important influences on my life were gained in those years when I worked and lived among the ranchers and cowboys of western Dakota and eastern Montana."[25]

His identification with the West made him more than just another parochial New York politician.

The pull of marriage and politics spurred Roosevelt's decision to leave the West. On a visit to New York in September 1885 he had renewed his acquaintance with Edith Carow at the home of his sister Anna. The couple began seeing each other and by November were secretly engaged. They agreed to marry in late 1886. Then Republicans in New York asked Theodore to run for mayor against the social reformer Henry George, of the United Labor Party, and the Democratic candidate, Abram S. Hewitt. Although he knew his chances of victory were slim, Roosevelt agreed, promising to "devote his whole energy to grappling actively with and rooting out the countless evils and abuses" in the city's government.[26] Despite his energetic campaign, however, Roosevelt ran a distant third. Few Republicans had expected him to win, but the race had further enhanced Roosevelt's standing as a promising young party newcomer.

Following the election, Roosevelt and Edith Carow were married in London on December 2, 1886. The best man was a young British diplomat, Cecil Spring Rice, whom Roosevelt had met on his wedding journey to England. "Springy" became a close friend and later a presidential back channel to the British government through Edith Roosevelt. The newlyweds brought little

Alice to live with them at Sagamore Hill, the hilltop house on Long Island Roosevelt had first envisioned as a home with his first wife. Roosevelt loved the rambling, over-stuffed mansion, which remained the family residence for the rest of his life.

Soon Theodore and Edith started their own family. Theodore Jr. arrived in September 1887, followed by Kermit (1889), Ethel (1891), Archibald (1894), and Quentin (1897). Edith brought calm and balance to her husband's life. In effect, she treated him as the oldest of her brood of unruly children. Relations with her step-daughter were more strained, especially when Alice emerged as a celebrity herself after her father became president.

The election of Benjamin Harrison as president in 1888 brought a Republican administration back to Washington. Roosevelt had stumped for the GOP ticket in the Midwest, and he hoped for an influential post in the new government. James G. Blaine, now secretary of state, turned down a proposal to name Roosevelt an assistant secretary. Ultimately the president appointed him to the Civil Service Commission, which seemed a safe place for Roosevelt to gain governmental experience in a minor federal post that did not shape policy.

Like other Republican politicians, Harrison had under-estimated Roosevelt's energy, reforming zeal, and instinct for the spotlight. The young commissioner pursued patronage misdeeds of both parties, including the transgressions of Harrison's postmaster general, John Wanamaker. To genteel reformers from Roosevelt's world, seeing that honest and upright individuals held office was a key to good government. In 1900, Harrison complained that Roosevelt had "wanted to put an end to all the evil in the world between sunrise and sunset."[27] What the president failed to grasp was that every controversy over the dry bones of patronage brought Roosevelt's name to the headlines.

During his six years in Washington, Roosevelt made many of the friends on whom his later career would turn—the historian Henry Adams, the future secretary of state John Hay, Speaker of the House Thomas B. Reed, and prominent foreign visitors such as the British historian and author of *The American Commonwealth*, James Bryce. One particular new acquaintance was William Howard Taft, whom Harrison named solicitor general in February 1890. Taft was in the capital for only two years before becoming a federal appeals court judge in Ohio. By 1894, Roosevelt was referring to him as "Judge Taft, of whom we are really fond."[28] Their wives, however, were less friendly.

After six years of overseeing how politicians handled the loaves and fishes of patronage, Roosevelt was looking for new political opportunities. With the Democrats in disarray across the nation because of the Panic of 1893, there was no point in remaining on the Civil Service Commission. He rebuffed Republican overtures to run for mayor of New York City in 1894, largely because of Edith's opposition. When William L. Strong carried the GOP to victory in the mayoral race, Roosevelt told friends that he would like to be one of the city's four police commissioners. His appointment came in April 1895. A month later he showed up at police headquarters at 300 Mulberry Street, with a gaggle of reporters trailing behind him, and asked: "Where are our offices? Where is the board room? What do we do first?"[29]

Elected president of the commission by his colleagues, Roosevelt added to his growing personal legend over the next two years. He went undercover through Manhattan's streets at night to find policemen sleeping on their beats or passing their working hours in saloons. Roosevelt's tenure on the police commission brought mixed results. He had to deal with the Democratic machine of Tammany Hall. He bickered with his fellow commissioners and encountered some Republican resistance when he pushed for enforcement of the state's liquor laws among German Americans. In two years he could not produce permanent changes in the culture of the police force, but he had shown what a vigorous executive could do to improve the performance of "New York's Finest."

By the end of 1896, however, his attention shifted back to national politics and the presidential candidacy of Republican William McKinley. He went out on the stump to denounce the Democratic candidate, William Jennings Bryan, and inveigh against his inflationary answers to the depression that had begun in 1893. Bryan's supporters, he proclaimed, constituted "the shiftless and vicious, and the honest but hopelessly ignorant and puzzle-headed voters."[30] If the GOP prevailed, Roosevelt hoped for a place in the new administration.

"I wish to heaven we were more jingo about Cuba and Hawaii!"[31]

When William McKinley won the presidency, Roosevelt believed that his campaigning had won him enough political credit for an important subcabinet post. Once again he enjoyed the strong support of Henry Cabot Lodge, now a senator from Massachusetts. Republican leaders in New York also liked the idea of the crusading Roosevelt being out of the state. Despite some reservations about his nominee's judgment and maturity, President McKinley selected him to be assistant secretary of the navy in April 1897.

Roosevelt served under Secretary of the Navy John Davis Long, who often found his energetic subordinate hard to handle. During his single year in office, the assistant secretary oversaw personnel matters and contributed to the readiness of the service when war with Spain came in 1898. Never an important policy maker in the McKinley government, Roosevelt gained the most attention for his public statements in favor of overseas expansion.

As the United States faced the question of whether to aid the popular insurrection against Spanish rule in Cuba, Roosevelt articulated an expansionist position. Influenced by the writings of Admiral Alfred T. Mahan on the importance of sea power, Roosevelt argued that the United States should oust the Spanish from Cuba and annex Hawaii. In a speech to the Naval War College on June 2, 1897, he proclaimed: "No triumph of peace is quite so great as the supreme triumphs of war."[32]

Roosevelt did not, however, create the tensions between Spain and the United States in 1897–98. Neither was he a large figure in the shaping and conduct of McKinley's foreign policy. Like most wars, the Spanish-American War occurred when two nations, both convinced that they were right, pursued their perceived national interests to a violent conclusion. Roosevelt prepared the American navy to meet the Spanish fleet, but he did not bring on the war.

Roosevelt is often credited with promoting American intervention in the Philippines once war began. When

Secretary Long left the office on February 25, 1898, Roosevelt wired George Dewey, the commander of an American squadron in the Pacific: "In the event of declaration of war on Spain, your duty will be to see that the Spanish squadron does not leave the Asiatic coast and then offensive operations in Philippine Islands."[33] From this telegram, the argument runs, flowed Dewey's victory at Manila Bay on May 1, 1898, American intervention and occupation of the archipelago, and the bloody Philippine Insurrection that followed.

The truth is more prosaic. Roosevelt's act was not that of an impetuous, imperialistic advocate of imperialism capitalizing on his chief's absence to advance a warlike agenda. The message reflected naval planning dating back to 1895 and one step in an ongoing process of preparation should hostilities occur. Secretary Long did not revoke the order when he came back the next day. More important, President McKinley issued the order for Dewey to attack on April 24, 1898, as the hostilities commenced.

Roosevelt's wife, Edith, was convalescing from serious surgery when the war broke out. President McKinley argued that an assistant secretary of the navy could contribute more to the war effort as an administrator than a soldier. But nothing was going to keep Roosevelt from donning a uniform. Remembering his father's failure to serve, he believed that he had to see combat to be true to his own principles. In addition, the legacy of the Civil War had sent Union officers from the military to the White House, such as President McKinley. Service in the conflict with Spain might produce the same result for an ambitious politician.

Roosevelt entered the army as a lieutenant colonel in a volunteer regiment commanded by Colonel Leonard Wood. Twenty-three thousand men volunteered for service in what the newspapers soon dubbed "Roosevelt's Rough Riders." By mid-May 1898 the regiment, with five hundred troops, along with its leader and its new second-in-command, were in San Antonio, Texas, to begin training.

Journalists loved the combination of Eastern aristocrats, western cowboys, and Native Americans that composed the Rough Riders. After a stay in Tampa, Florida, the regiment sailed to Cuba in mid-June, disembarked a week later, and first encountered the enemy in a skirmish at a spot called Las Guasimas on June 24. By the morning of July 1, 1898, the Rough Riders were ready to join an American assault on the San Juan Heights surrounding the city. Roosevelt was now a colonel and the commander of the regiment after Wood's promotion to brigadier general.

Following a morning of intense fighting, Roosevelt received orders in the early afternoon to assault the hills in front of his lines. Kettle Hill lay ahead, and, leading then on horseback, he took his men through the lines of U.S. Army regulars and up the slope. Jumping off his horse halfway up, he ran forward, killing at least one Spaniard. From the top of Kettle Hill, he joined the charge on the remaining San Juan Heights. "Look at all those damned Spanish dead," he told a comrade. Four years later he lamented that "the only trouble" in the war with Spain "was that there was not enough war to go around."[34] His experience in Cuba convinced him that he had the military skill and knowledge to serve in future wars in a similar commanding role.

In the siege of Santiago that ensued and lasted until the Spanish surrendered, Roosevelt collaborated with other officers to warn Washington and the nation of the dangers of disease if the army stayed in Cuba. When he returned home in August 1898, Roosevelt received popular acclaim. Political opportunity beckoned. New York Republicans faced a tough gubernatorial election with a scandal and an incumbent who was losing political support daily. Having a war hero and champion of imperialism at the top of ticket appealed to the party's rank and file. Roosevelt assured the Republican boss, Senator Thomas Collier Platt, that he would consult the GOP organization on policy. Meanwhile, the prospective candidate fended off challenges about whether his legal residence was in New York or Washington. Roosevelt got the nomination and hit the campaign trail with a contingent of Rough Riders beside him. His speeches emphasized his recent feats in Cuba. One former Rough Rider informed an audience that Roosevelt "told us we might meet wounds and death and we done it, but he was thar in the midst of us, and when it comes to the great day he led us up San Juan Hill like sheep to the slaughter and so he will lead you." He secured a narrow 17,000-vote victory over his Democratic opponent. At the age of forty, Roosevelt was governor of the largest state of the Union and a potential presidential candidate in 1904.[35]

Roosevelt's two years as governor of New York foreshadowed many of the achievements of his presidency. Daily press conferences kept the public informed about the activities of a dynamic young chief executive. He worked with Senator Platt and party regulars as much as possible, but he went his own way in some appointments, as well as on conservation policy. His support of greater publicity (what would now be called "transparency") about corporate affairs as a means of regulating big business carried over into his early years in the White House. Even those mild steps toward regulating business disturbed the rich men on whom Senator Platt relied for campaign funds and machine operations. By 1900 Roosevelt felt growing pressure from both his admirers and critics to seek higher office. Nonetheless, at the end of his term in Albany, he could say:

"I think I have been the best Governor within my time, better than either Cleveland or [Samuel J.] Tilden."[36]

William McKinley's vice president, Garret Hobart, had died in November 1899. Friends of Roosevelt argued that he was the logical choice to run with the president in 1900. Roosevelt wanted to keep his options open for 1904. He hoped to gain executive experience by becoming secretary of war, but that post went to Elihu Root. Governor of the Philippines was also appealing, but William Howard Taft was chosen for that assignment. Another term as governor seemed the remaining alternative, even though he would leave office in 1902 without a base from which to launch a campaign for the Republican nomination. Despite its apparent political insignificance as a stepping stone to the White House, the vice presidency was the most available national post the Republicans had open that year.

Roosevelt said all the right things to take himself out of the race without issuing an unequivocal declaration that would have put him beyond the reach of a genuine draft. Despite his public disclaimers, in the end western enthusiasm for him, Senator Platt's eagerness to remove him from New York, and the absence of a credible alternative made him the logical vice presidential choice. Had he stayed away from the national convention in Philadelphia, he might have avoided being nominated.

But then some other contender might have been named and jumped ahead of him in the race to succeed McKinley in 1904. Wearing his Rough Rider hat and evoking enthusiasm from the delegates who saw him as a guarantee of victory, Roosevelt headed for Philadelphia. Once he was present in the hall, he succumbed to "the intoxication of the hurrah of the crowd."[37] The ticket of McKinley and Roosevelt, with the vice presidential candidate doing the active campaigning, routed William Jennings Bryan and the Democrats in the election of 1900. "There is nothing whatever in the vice-presidency as an office, and I should infinitely rather have been Governor for two more years than vice-president for four," Roosevelt told Cecil Spring Rice, adding, "I shall enjoy my new place too."[38]

When Roosevelt was nominated, Senator Marcus A. Hanna wrote to his close friend President McKinley: "Your *duty* to the Country is to *live* for *four* years from next March."[39] At first it seemed that Roosevelt had been kicked upstairs in satisfactory fashion. But he was soon bored with the minimal duties of presiding over the Senate. Meanwhile, his friends had started to gather commitments for a try for the Republican nomination in 1904. Asked in July 1901 if he would run, Roosevelt replied, "Certainly, if the people want me. It's the highest aim a young man can have."[40]

In September 1901, President McKinley went to the Pan-American Exposition in Buffalo, New York, where he was struck by an assassin's bullet on September 6. He died on September 14, and Theodore Roosevelt became the twenty-sixth chief executive. At forty-two, he was the youngest president then and since. He issued a statement that he would "continue absolutely unbroken" McKinley's policies. Friends said that Roosevelt "really is a man of destiny" and wondered "how those who thought to shelve him with the Vice-Presidency now feel." Republicans were soon reporting, "The new President is starting off well and is showing his independence of character at every opportunity. He says to his friends quietly but firmly: 'I will be President.' "[41]

"It is a dreadful thing to come into the Presidency in this way but it would be a far worse thing to be morbid about it."[42]

William McKinley had already set the presidency on its modern course, but Roosevelt added key dramatic elements of his own. He brought to his new job a zest for governing and a sense of fun that enthralled the American public. Roosevelt did not complain about the burdens of his office; he reveled in the responsibility of leading the nation. For eight years, in a time of peace and relative prosperity, he mixed serious policy deliberations with a capacity to entertain. A friend dubbed him "the meteor of the age." When the president was "in the neighborhood," wrote one of his newspaper critics, the public could "no more look the other way than the small boy can turn his head away from a circus parade followed by a steam calliope."[43]

He changed the official name of the residence from the Executive Mansion to the White House, encouraged even wider press coverage of the presidency than McKinley had, and spent much time on the road seeing his fellow Americans. "I have got such a bully pulpit," he said toward the end of his tenure, and he preached to the American people on everything from football to simplified spelling. The public read that the president exercised daily, played with members of his "Tennis Cabinet" on a White House court, and exhausted politicians and diplomats on horseback rides and strenuous walks around Washington. When the president declined to shoot a trapped bear during a hunting trip in Mississippi in 1902, a cartoonist created the teddy bear, and an enduring American toy was born. "The two things in America which seem to me most extraordinary," said the English writer and politician John Morley, "are Niagara Falls and Prest Roosevelt."[44]

Roosevelt's whole family became national news. Reporters talked of "the White House Gang" of presidential offspring and tracked the summer goings-on of the clan at the family home named Sagamore Hill. The most famous of the Roosevelt progeny was Alice Lee, a debutante, owner of a pet snake called Emily Spinach, and devotee of cigarettes and fast cars. Her marriage to Representative Nicholas Longworth, an Ohio Republican, became the talk of the nation in 1906. When the novelist Owen Wister asked the president to control his daughter, Roosevelt replied: "I can be President of the United States—or—I can attend to Alice."[45]

Roosevelt's personality and demeanor captivated the nation. He stood five feet eight and weighed two hundred pounds. His trademark mustache, prominent teeth, and sturdy and distinctive features made him easy to caricature in a cartoon. Visitors expecting a frenetic chief executive were surprised at how calm the president seemed. "His nerves are so steady that he doesn't even twirl his fingers," wrote a journalist in 1904, "and if you will note closely you will see that not a muscle of his features twitches." An active mind meant that Roosevelt dominated conversations, often finishing his guests' sentences for them. As his friend, the Kansas editor William Allen White, observed to a politician going to see the president, "Now talking with Roosevelt often does no good, because he does all the talking. But when you write to him and he can't talk back, you get a chance to put in more."[46]

Courting the press became a central pursuit of the Roosevelt presidency. Reporters already had a designated work space on the second floor of the White House. Roosevelt provided them with a press room of their own. There were no regular press conferences, but news came out when journalists chatted with the president while he was being shaved in the afternoon. If a story was published that Roosevelt did not like, he would relegate the offending scribe to the "Ananias Club," named after the biblical liar, and cut off access to the reporter. The president's secretary, William Loeb, engaged in a good deal of manipulation of reporting. "The President is a great 'news man,' but he wants to give out the news himself—to control the source of information," commented a Washington correspondent in 1906.[47]

> **"After combinations had reached a certain stage it is indispensable to the general welfare that the Nation should exercise over them, cautiously and with self-restraint, but firmly, the power of supervision and regulation."[48]**

Roosevelt did not come to the White House with a well-developed program of action on domestic issues, but in his first year he made two striking departures from previous economic policies. In February 1902, the

Department of Justice filed an antitrust suit against the Northern Securities Company, a combination of three major railroads in the Northwest that sought to dominate the market in that region. Roosevelt believed that the federal government should be superior to any private economic power, and he used the Sherman Antitrust Act of 1890 to break up the railroad empire. The president did not like the Sherman Act as a long-range economic principle, but he was convinced that "the great corporations which we have grown to speak of rather loosely as trusts are the creatures of the State, and the State not only has the right to control, but it is in duty bound to control them wherever the need of such control is shown."[49]

A Supreme Court decision in 1904 upheld the government's position and confirmed Roosevelt's victory. A pleased president had established "the newer and more wholesome doctrine under which the Federal Government may now deal with monopolistic combinations and conspiracies." Once the principle of government supremacy had been affirmed, Roosevelt turned to informed, expert regulation of business through the Bureau of Corporations (1903), a forerunner of the Federal Trade Commission.[50]

A major labor dispute offered Roosevelt the opportunity to wield presidential power to resolve an economic crisis in the autumn of 1902. Miners in the anthracite coal regions had walked off their jobs the previous summer. With winter coming, the nation confronted an urgent fuel crisis. Previous presidents had used troops to break strikes, most notably Grover Cleveland in 1894. Rather than intervene on the side of management, Roosevelt took the unprecedented step of summoning owners and miners to the White House to forge a settlement. Roosevelt's pressure produced an agreement, ending the walkout and laying the foundation for similar executive action in future labor confrontations. The president had a name for his even-handed policies: the Square Deal. Treating capital and labor on the same basis was one of his important innovations.

Roosevelt's success as a trust buster and labor mediator boosted his popularity, but a 1903 triumph in foreign policy all but insured his election to the presidency in 1904. Despite his historical image as an impulsive seeker after military confrontations, Roosevelt in office was a cautious, temperate diplomatic leader. As he told an audience in Chicago in April 1903, "There is a homely old adage which runs 'Speak softly and carry a big stick; you will go far.'"[51] Far from seeking war, Roosevelt was reluctant to engage in armed intervention. In the Philippines, he had to deal with the continuing effects of the insurrection against American rule that began in 1899 and was largely subdued by 1901. Outside of that military involvement, the president sent no Americans into combat during his two terms.

In securing the Panama Canal Zone, however, Roosevelt provided fodder for critics of his foreign policy style. The effort to build a canal across Central America antedated Roosevelt's administration. By 1902 the United States had decided on engineering grounds that construction across the Isthmus of Panama was preferable to a route through Nicaragua. Roosevelt negotiated a treaty with Colombia, the nation then sovereign over Panama, to construct a canal. However, the Colombian Congress refused to ratify the treaty as an infringement on the nation's sovereignty, in hopes of securing more money from Washington. Roosevelt did not believe that "the Bogota lot of jack rabbits should be allowed permanently to bar one of the future highways of civilization."[52]

To achieve his goal, Roosevelt encouraged, but did not foment, a revolution of the Panamanians and their American supporters. The presence of American ships near Panama in early November 1903, dispatched there by the president, helped make the uprising a success. The State Department negotiated a treaty giving the United States a zone within Panama. The United States acquired virtual sovereignty over the zone and very favorable rental terms. Democrats charged that Roosevelt had misused his power to accomplish acquisition of the Canal Zone, but the American people cheered the result. The Northern Securities antitrust case, the anthracite coal strike, and the Panama episode had made Roosevelt the odds-on favorite for election in his own right.

"I think I can truthfully say that I now have to my credit a sum of substantial achievement and the rest must take care of itself."[53]

Theodore Roosevelt looked to the 1904 presidential election with a mixture of optimism and foreboding. Political circumstances seemed bright for the Republicans. The country was prosperous, the Democrats were disorganized, and Roosevelt enjoyed popularity everywhere. By 1902 it was evident that he would receive his party's nomination. Yet, with characteristic pessimism, the president worried that he might face a challenge from Senator Hanna, the leader of Republican conservatives. The result was a struggle for control of the Grand Old Party in 1903 in which Roosevelt held all the high cards. By the time Hanna died in February 1904, it was clear that Roosevelt had prevailed, and his nomination at the national convention in June was assured. Any opposition to his candidacy in the Midwest and elsewhere was "disappearing like the mist before the sun."[54]

Meanwhile, the Democrats struggled to find a nominee to challenge Roosevelt. After two losing races in 1896 and 1900, William Jennings Bryan had decided not to try again in 1904. Instead, the Democrats sought a conservative candidate who could be contrasted with Roosevelt's impetuous and activist reputation. A decision to run to the right of the president made little sense, but the desperate Democratic conservatives thought that their risky initiative might work. They selected a New York State Court of Appeals judge named Alton B. Parker, a colorless, safe conservative who, as one newspaper put it, presented "to the inquiring vision all the salient qualities of a sphere."⁵⁵

The Democratic strategy relied on the votes of the "Solid South," where the party commanded support because of the legacy of the Civil War and the race issue. They planned to add to that base the presumed ability of Parker to carry New York (based on his successful race for the state bench in 1897 and taking no account of Roosevelt's strength in his home state). With the Empire State won for Parker, success in another few states such as Indiana would produce electoral victory. It was a long-shot approach that never had a chance against Roosevelt's popularity. Parker proved to be a lackluster candidate. While Roosevelt, as an incumbent, observed tradition and did not campaign, he never really needed to go out on the hustings. "This is the

most apathetic campaign ever heard of since James Monroe's second election," wrote one magazine editor. The quiet canvass was "as different from what we are accustomed to in September and October of a presidential year as black is different from white."[56]

The campaign was dull right up to the end, when Parker complained that the Republicans were pressuring corporations to make campaign contributions "to buy protection" from Roosevelt and his party. The charge contained a significant element of truth, but Parker did not have definite proof of what he was alleging. Roosevelt issued vehement denials in a series of public statements, promising, "I shall see to it that every man has a square deal, no less and no more."[57]

The voters responded with a true landslide victory. Roosevelt received 56.4 percent of the popular vote, with 37.6 percent for Parker. The president carried thirty-three of the forty-five states and won 336 electoral votes, the most in any election up to that time. The election-night waiting was over early, and then Roosevelt pulled another one of his frequent surprises. He gathered the press corps around him and said that his time already served in office "constituted my first term. The wise custom which limits the President to two terms regards the substance and not the form. Under no circumstances will I be a candidate for or accept another nomination."[58]

Roosevelt had not decided in haste to make this self-denying pledge. He had discussed the option with several friends in the days before making the announcement to the reporters. William McKinley had issued such a statement in the summer of 1901, and the 1904 pledge was also designed to deflect charges that Roosevelt was an incipient dictator. On the night of his election he had removed the possibility that he might be a candidate in 1908, and he later reemphasized his lame-duck status toward the end of the second term. However, he regretted that he had made such a vow before he left the White House, and it hampered his chances in 1912.

For the moment, basking in the warmth of his emphatic endorsement, Roosevelt looked toward implementing an ambitious program in domestic reform and foreign policy. His most productive years as an activist president lay ahead.

"That we shall have a muss on the interstate commerce business next year I have no doubt; but I feel that we can get the issue so clearly drawn that the Senate will have to give in."[59]

As Theodore Roosevelt began his second term, his country was experiencing the effects of a movement for political reform that people both at the time and since have labeled "progressivism." This campaign for political change was born in the depression of the 1890s in the cities and states and spread to the national scene during the first five years of the twentieth century. Roosevelt emerged as the first president to champion progressive reform.

Two broad themes defined what many middle-class Americans and their allies were seeking. In response to the social problems arising from the rapid industrialization of the late nineteenth century, the progressives argued that government regulation offered a middle course between unbridled capitalism and the government ownership and control that socialists advocated. A second drive was to make national politics more democratic through such devices as primary elections, woman suffrage, the ballot initiative (through which the people could propose legislation), referendum (to seek popular votes on disputed issues), and recall (removing unpopular officials or overturning judicial decisions). The direct election of United States senators by the people of a state also was part of the progressive agenda. This reform impulse mixed positive and negative elements, but much of what it sought accorded with the aims of Theodore Roosevelt during his second term.

Roosevelt recognized that the government could not remain passive in the face of the problems that reformers identified. There were inequities that needed attention.

Railroads wielded a heavy hand in the economy. Consumers faced the hazards of patent medicines and tainted meat products. Industrial accidents crippled workers. Child labor was a widespread evil. No system of old age pensions, health insurance, or unemployment insurance existed. Corruption stained state legislatures and the Congress. Roosevelt exemplified a generation that addressed the weaknesses of American society with a broad-ranging campaign for what that era called "uplift."

Three legislative enactments came out of Roosevelt's heightened effort to use national power for economic change. The most significant was the Hepburn Act of 1906, which broadened the power of the Interstate Commerce Commission to regulate railroad rates. Roosevelt wielded all the power of the presidency to secure passage of this measure. He made speaking tours on behalf of railroad control, his administration played a large role in drafting the measure, and he acted as a de facto member of the Senate in pushing the bill through during the first half of 1906. Despite strong resistance from Senate conservatives, the president obtained much of what he sought. It was, he wrote, "a fine piece of constructive legislation, and all that has been done tends toward carrying out the principles I have been preaching."[60]

As railroad regulation gathered momentum, two other related issues arose. Upton Sinclair's best-selling novel *The*

Jungle called popular attention to unsanitary and disgusting conditions in the nation's stockyards. A clamor arose for federal supervision of these facilities. Roosevelt worked with sympathetic lawmakers to include a meat-inspection amendment in agriculture appropriations legislation. The final bill was not as strong as it could have been, but it represented an important first step toward safer meat. Finally, crusading journalists had exposed unsafe practices in the patent medicine industry and the preparation of packaged foods. The president threw his support behind the Pure Food and Drug Act, which reached his desk during that same period of legislative action. That too was enacted in a burst of legislation that made that session of Congress the most consequential of Roosevelt's presidency. He called the three measures "a noteworthy advance in the policy of securing Federal supervision and control over corporations."[61]

"We were at absolute peace, and there was no nation in the world with whom a war cloud threatened, and no nation in the world whom we had wronged or from who we had anything to fear."[62]

For all his love of the spotlight, Roosevelt favored quiet diplomacy and confidential negotiations in the handling of foreign affairs. His second term demonstrated those qualities as he set in motion important innovations in American diplomacy. Using the formal instruments of foreign policy as well as private ties with such English friends as Spring Rice and the soldier-politician Arthur Lee, Roosevelt sought to expand his country's role in world affairs.

When war broke out between Russia and Japan in 1904, Roosevelt saw the United States as the logical mediator. Tilting toward Tokyo and suspicious of Russian aims in the area, the president worked in private to get the two sides to the peace table. In the spring of 1905 a Russian naval defeat and the war-weariness of Tokyo persuaded both belligerents that it was in their interest to negotiate a peace. Gathering at Portsmouth, New Hampshire, in the late summer of 1905, the Japanese and Russian envoys hammered out a settlement, with Roosevelt much involved in the proceedings. The Peace of Portsmouth ended the fighting, though it left the Japanese angry at the Americans for depriving them of the imagined spoils of their victories in battle.

During that same summer, Tokyo and Washington probed each others' contrasting positions about the balance of power in Asia. In what became known as the Taft-Katsura Agreement, but which was only a statement of the positions of Washington and Tokyo in mid-1905, the United States acquiesced to Japanese supremacy in the Korean peninsula, while Japan disclaimed any intentions to attack the Philippines. The handling of the Korean episode left that small nation under Japanese dominance, but the United States lacked the will and the resources to have stopped Tokyo. Aware that the new American possession of the Philippines could not be defended and was "our heel of Achilles," Roosevelt recognized that public opinion would not support aggressive efforts to forestall Japan's expansion. His answer was to maintain the readiness of the American navy, to limit the commitment to the Philippines, and to accept Japanese dominance in Korea and Manchuria.[63]

In 1906, California sought to segregate the children of Japanese immigrants within the public school system. The racial distinction inherent in this policy outraged Japanese officials and their public. The press in the United States talked of possible war with Japan. To avoid further tension, Roosevelt and Japan negotiated an informal "Gentleman's Agreement" in 1907 to limit the flow of Japanese immigrants. To show American naval strength, the president sent battleships of the "Great White Fleet" (a reference to the peacetime white paint of the vessels) around the world. When they returned in early 1909, Roosevelt exulted in the display of naval strength and the success of his policy.

Roosevelt also broadened the role of the United States in European affairs when he had the nation participate, in an informal manner, in the Algeciras Conference on the fate of Morocco in 1906. The episode threatened a European war between France and Germany. Keeping the Germans friendly, Roosevelt tilted toward the interests of France and helped secure the settlement of an international crisis that Berlin and the kaiser had precipitated. Roosevelt was careful not to go beyond what public opinion at home would accept, but nonetheless he sought to preserve peace in Europe.

In Latin America, the second term brought the enunciation of the Roosevelt Corollary to the Monroe Doctrine in 1904. If countries in that region failed to honor their international debts, the United States would act. "Chronic wrongdoing," wrote Roosevelt, might compel the United States "in flagrant cases of such wrong-doing or impotence, to the exercise of an international police power."[64] Applied first to the Dominican Republic, the Corollary implied that the United States possessed a greater innate political capacity to sustain civilization than did its neighbors in Latin America. The creed of the Corollary seemed to its critics a prime example of imperialism and bluster.

When he left office in March 1909, Roosevelt believed he had been a good steward of the national interest in foreign policy. His trip to Panama in 1906 to inspect canal construction had broken the precedent of presidents remaining inside the United States while in office. He had been an effective peacemaker, and he had reminded Americans of their widening role in a dangerous world.

"The relation of the conservation of natural resources to the problems of national welfare and national efficiency had not yet dawned on the public mind."[65]

Roosevelt used his bully pulpit to shape public opinion on many subjects. Conservation of natural resources received special emphasis, as did the state of the nation's race relations. Earlier presidents had done little to protect scenic places and national parks against the wasteful exploitation of the environment. His main ally within the government was Gifford Pinchot, the chief forester. Roosevelt persuaded Congress in 1905 to move complete responsibility for the national forests from the Interior Department to Pinchot's agency, the Forest Service, in the Department of Agriculture. The two men proved a capable team. The president achieved much, creating five national parks, four national game preserves, fifty-one bird reservations, and one hundred and fifty national forests. Major legislation included the Newlands Reclamation Act (1902) and the Antiquities Act (1906). He sought to shape future resource programs with the creation of the

Inland Waterways Commission (1907) and the National Governors' Conference on Conservation (1908).

Roosevelt's warnings about the degradation of the natural world may seem very modern. His answers in his own day, however, relied on business support and reflected a top-down approach to decision making about resources. He and Pinchot cooperated with large corporations in shaping policy and issued directives on grazing, waterways, and forests from Washington. They often overrode local interests. As a result, their conservation campaigns provoked western opposition and the criticism that the president and his aides often acted beyond the law. One instance came in early 1907 when western senators enacted language to limit the executive's power to establish forest reserves. Working at top speed with Pinchot, the president issued proclamations creating twenty-one new reserves on March 2, 1907, two days before the legislation took effect. Roosevelt relied on the implied powers of the executive to justify his actions in the public interest as he defined that elusive concept. While his commitment to the out-of-doors was genuine and important in shaping public attitudes, the methods used to accomplish his ends limited the long-range impact of his policies.

On racial matters, Roosevelt thought of himself as the heir to Abraham Lincoln. In fact, he followed the segregationist customs of that era and showed little of Lincoln's capacity for growth. He doubted the ability of black Americans to govern themselves without white supervision. His first action in October 1901 was to invite the prominent black leader Booker T. Washington to dine at the White House. The subject of the conversation was not civil rights; Roosevelt consulted Washington about Republican patronage in the South to secure the support of black delegates to the 1904 national convention. When the news of the social event became public, southern newspapers erupted with denunciations of Roosevelt's breach of the color line. Although he supported the appointment of several African Americans to federal offices in the South during his first term, Roosevelt backed away from any effort to increase the number of black officials in the government. He also warned blacks that they should turn in criminals from their community to keep whites from resorting to lynching.

When a shooting occurred in Brownsville, Texas, in August 1906, the president blamed African American soldiers stationed there and dismissed dozens of the men from the army without a trial or a chance to defend themselves. He never changed his mind about his role in what was a miscarriage of justice, and he punished political opponents such as Senator Joseph B. Foraker who defended the accused troops. It was his worst abuse of presidential power in domestic affairs.

"You blessed old trump. I have always said you [William Howard Taft] would be the greatest President bar only Washington and Lincoln, and I feel mighty inclined to strike out the exceptions!"[66]

Having pledged not to run in 1908, Roosevelt then determined that he would have a major hand in the selection of his successor. One moment of self-denial was enough. Over the next two years, he came to believe that his secretary of war, William Howard Taft, would be the best choice for the GOP. If his secretary of state, Elihu Root, had not been so identified with a law practice for corporate clients and seemed old for the presidency (though he would outlive Roosevelt and Taft), the president might well have designated him. With Root out of the running, Taft became the most likely successor.

In making his choice, Roosevelt overlooked the ways in which he and Taft disagreed about the reach of executive power and the proper role for the president. A lawyer by profession with a more conservative mindset than his friend, Taft valued the letter of statutes and the limits of presidential authority, whereas Roosevelt saw himself as the steward of the people. If the Constitution did not forbid the president from exercising his prerogatives, Roosevelt felt free to act. Taft preferred to remain within accustomed limits and not to stretch the Constitution. Either the two men did not find occasions to explore their principled differences or else they simply avoided anything that might be a touchy topic.

Once he had decided on Taft over other rivals, Roosevelt told himself that his political heir was not just the best candidate available but one of the finest prospective presidents in all of American history. "He and I view public questions exactly alike," said the president with typical overstatement.[67] Roosevelt oversold Taft to himself with predictable disappointment when Taft fell short of the ideal. Soon after Taft won the nomination in June 1908, the two men drifted apart over matters large and small. By the time that Taft had defeated William Jennings Bryan in November 1908, Roosevelt was enthusiastic in public, but personal qualms lingered about his successor.

Roosevelt believed that Taft had promised to retain the members of his cabinet. The president-elect thought that some of the officials needed to be replaced. One small episode in particular had significant consequences. Days after the election Taft wrote to Roosevelt to thank him for his role in elevating him to the White House. "You and my brother Charlie made that possible which in all probability would not have occurred otherwise."[68]

Charles P. Taft, the president-elect's half brother and a wealthy Ohio newspaper owner, had bankrolled much of the campaign. In Roosevelt's mind, to compare his efforts with those of Charles Taft was like saying that "Abraham Lincoln and the bond-seller Jay Cooke saved the Union."[69] That Roosevelt was so sensitive about what was meant as a gracious thank-you letter indicates how tenuous his links with Taft were as power passed from one man to another. Tension between Edith Roosevelt and Helen Taft added to the strain as Inauguration Day approached in March 1909.

For the public and political commentators in the press, Roosevelt's last weeks in office were a time of reflection about what his presidency had meant to the nation. He had broadened the agenda of national affairs, increased the power of his office, and brought forward the question of government regulation of the economy. Above all, he had added a spirit of excitement and energy to the everyday process of politics. As he told his oldest son, "I have been full President right up to the end—which hardly any other President ever has been." He was, the editors of a popular magazine wrote, "the happiest man that ever dwelt in the White House."[70]

After Taft took over, Roosevelt planned to leave for Africa with his son Kermit for a safari of hunting and acquiring African plants and animals on behalf of the

Smithsonian Institution. Such a trip would insulate him from charges that he was directing Taft's policies from outside the government. He also hoped that it might lessen excessive popular interest in his daily activities.

He bequeathed to Taft a Republican party that was divided over its future direction. Progressives wanted to see the reforms of the Roosevelt years extended and broadened. Conservatives believed that Roosevelt had gone too far toward government regulation, and they looked for Taft to retrench. The outgoing president shared the progressive impulses of Pinchot, James R. Garfield, and others who had formed his Tennis Cabinet in the White House. They looked to the incoming president to continue the programs started under Roosevelt. "If Taft weakens," wrote Senator Joseph L. Bristow of Kansas, "he will annihilate himself."[71]

During his White House years, Roosevelt had become accustomed to the perquisites of the nation's highest office in dealing with his personal and professional needs. On March 4, 1909, he reverted to the status of private citizen in an era when former presidents received no pension, had no Secret Service protection, and could not count on any office staff or professional support. The youngest ex-president since Ulysses S. Grant in 1877, Roosevelt found himself the most famous living American, with all the demands of fame and none of the resources to cope with his celebrity. With his usual insight into his friend's situation, Elihu Root observed, "[Roosevelt] may try to act like a private citizen but of course he cannot possibly help being a public character for the rest of his life."[72]

"I am living in an unspeakable world, and heartily long to be back at Sagamore Hill."[73]

The nature of a public figure was also changing at the time Roosevelt returned to private life for the first time in twenty years. The growth of the motion picture industry had awakened in the public a "vast unsatisfied curiosity" about the actors in cinematic dramas.[74] The concept of stardom emerged to explain the attraction of players such as Charlie Chaplin and Mary Pickford who commanded salaries of several thousand dollars per week. Fan magazines retailed news stories, some real, some invented, about these charismatic performers. They enjoyed an ambiguous connection to the public that adored them at times and rejected them at others. The ways in which entertainment was covered in the press soon spilled over into how political figures were followed.

The man who left for Africa in March 1909 was thus a star in his own right who, now out of office, was "known for his well knowness."[75] In dealing with his new status as the object of media fixation, Roosevelt also had to contend with the lingering physical effects of the presidency even as the public was unaware of the price he had paid. With Roosevelt's penchant for indulging in rich desserts, his weight had increased until he was closer in heft to the rotund Taft than popular impressions would have suggested. He took no rest after the demands of office but plunged into preparations to leave for Africa three weeks later. He expected that the insatiable press interest in his activities would ease once he was in private life. Much to his surprise and dismay, the fascination with his activities would intensify once the protective shield of the presidency had been removed.

The problem for Roosevelt was that he lacked a secure source of income in presidential retirement. To support his large family and affluent lifestyle, he returned to writing for magazines. He arranged with the *Outlook* magazine to be a contributing editor at $25,000 per year. In that capacity he commented over the next four years on a diverse range of topics from medieval poetry to the future of Alaska.

What sold issues of the magazine and kept Roosevelt in the public arena, however, was the possibility that he might run for president again in 1912 or 1916. If he simply endorsed President Taft's policies and became just another Republican elder statesman, the audience for his prose would soon disappear, along with his writing income. Supporting Taft for renomination, for example, would have drained all suspense from Roosevelt's public commentary. To make a living Roosevelt needed to maintain his political stardom. A man of restless temperament, with ideas about the nation's direction, he chafed at inactivity and isolation. He might proclaim his desire for peace and quiet, but when there were dips in his fame he soon became restive and eager to return to the political fray. Running for president became his post–White House profession.

The ramifications of the strong public fascination with Roosevelt emerged during his African hunting trip and European tour in 1909–10. There were fabricated interviews and bogus accounts of what he was doing on safari. Some obviously faked movies, one of them shot in California, depicted the former president in the wild. To satisfy popular demand, Roosevelt recruited a friendly reporter, Warrington Dawson, to recount the progress of the hunt for the press corps. When Roosevelt returned first to Europe and then home in the spring of 1910, it was to intense popular acclaim everywhere. In Hungary, for example, "the broad street running alongside the Danube was filled which a dense crowd which cheered, and cheered, and only ceased when he appeared and cordially expressed his thanks for the demonstration."[76]

While he was hunting and fending off admirers, Roosevelt allowed his relationship with Taft to deteriorate further. The two men did not correspond while Roosevelt was away. Whether each expected the other to act first is not clear, but they did not keep in touch except through third parties. Instead, Roosevelt heard from his progressive allies about Taft's alleged failings with the tariff, conservation, and railroad regulation. When Taft fired Gifford Pinchot in January 1910 for insubordination in a dispute over conservation policy with Secretary of the Interior Richard A. Ballinger, Roosevelt felt a deep sense of personal betrayal. The Ballinger-Pinchot dispute became emblematic of Roosevelt's disillusion with the leadership of the man he had put into the presidency. The controversy also highlighted the differences between the two presidents regarding the proper extent of executive power.

Rather than write to his successor and ask what was going on, Roosevelt brooded about Taft's weaknesses and his own misjudgment in selecting him as his heir. In May 1910, on the eve of his return home, he wrote, "I ... [have] to admit to myself that deep down underneath I had known all along" that Taft was "wrong, on points as to which I had tried to deceive myself, by loudly proclaiming to myself that he was right."[77] He turned down an invitation from the president to visit the White House on the implausible grounds that former presidents should not do so.

Upon his arrival in New York City on June 18, 1910, Roosevelt received a tumultuous welcome from crowds that lined the streets to cheer him at every corner. Buoyed by his reception, the former president told the cluster of reporters pressing him for a statement that he would have nothing to say about politics then or later. Within a short time, however, he had plunged back into New York politics at the behest of the state's governor, Charles Evans Hughes. It seemed safe to do so since he and Taft were on the same side, but any involvement in Republican affairs stirred speculation that Roosevelt might challenge the president in 1912.

Opponents of Taft came to see Roosevelt at Oyster Bay, much to the annoyance of the White House. There were two rival camps within the Republican Party as the off-year election of 1910 neared. An informal meeting of Taft and Roosevelt on June 30, 1910, with others present, brought no progress in resolving the substantive quarrels between the two onetime friends. In their private letters, they spoke more of their differences than their days of friendship.

Roosevelt then raised the stakes for 1912 with an important statement about the proper direction of national reform among Republicans. Responding to calls from progressives for help in the congressional elections, Roosevelt made a speaking tour of the West in August and September 1910. In Kansas, he called for a "New Nationalism" that went beyond the Square Deal of his presidency. "When I say that I am for the square deal, I mean not merely that I stand for fair play under the present rules of the game, but that I stand for having those rules changed so as to work for a more substantial equality of opportunity and of reward for equally good service." He advocated graduated income and inheritance taxes on great fortunes, limits on corporate influence on politics, and laws to regulate child labor and provide for workmen's compensation.[78] He was repeating positions he had taken in messages to Congress at the end of his presidency, but his attacks on judges, calls for social legislation, and more radical tone in general rattled Republican conservatives.

> **"Taft was a first-class lieutenant; but he is only fit to act under orders; and for three years and a half the orders given him have been wrong. Now he has lost his temper and is behaving like a blackguard."[79]**

In the short run, Roosevelt's efforts could not prevent the Republicans from experiencing serious reverses in the 1910 elections. Roosevelt's hand-picked candidate for governor of New York, Henry L. Stimson, lost in an embarrassing defeat for the former president. After the Republicans' trouncing at the polls, Taft and Roosevelt enjoyed a brief rekindling of their friendship, but the harmony did not last. There were more calls from progressives for Roosevelt to challenge the president in 1912. For the moment, however, Roosevelt fended off these entreaties.

His position changed in late October 1911 when Taft's Justice Department filed an antitrust suit against the United States Steel Corporation. In its pleading the government claimed that Roosevelt had been duped in 1907 when, during a banking crisis, he allowed U.S. Steel to acquire a competing firm as a way of calming fears on Wall Street. An outraged Roosevelt denounced the suit and, along with it, Taft's economic policies. He listened with more attention to friends who told him he should run for president. If these allies could demonstrate a popular sentiment for his nomination, he would regard it as his duty to enter the race. Soon evidence of a boom for Roosevelt echoed across the nation. The enthusiasm for Roosevelt overshadowed the hopes of the other progressive Republican in the contest, Senator Robert M. La Follette of Wisconsin.

While there were policy differences with Taft that in Roosevelt's mind justified running, personal elements played a large part in the decision. Private life bored him, and only in the White House had he felt fulfilled. Wiser heads said to wait until 1916. Elihu Root later recalled, "If Roosevelt could only have put his feet on the mantelpiece for a little while, the whole world would have come to him. But he could not keep his feet off the floor—he could not stop dancing for a minute." Roosevelt wanted to reenter the fray and seek vindication for his programs and another lease on power. "My hat is in the ring, the fight is on, and I am stripped to the buff," Roosevelt told reporters on February 21, 1912.[80]

Roosevelt's willingness to be a candidate raised the third-term issue against him among moderate and conservative Republicans. To a significant portion of his party, moreover, Roosevelt seemed a power-mad radical lusting for a return to the highest office in the land. As a bitter fight for the GOP nomination got under way in the winter of 1912, these Republicans rushed to support Taft.

The way in which Roosevelt launched his White House race diminished his early momentum as a candidate. Long suspicious of the judiciary as a check on progressive programs, he argued that voters should have the right to cast their ballots on state court rulings that overturned state laws. This "recall of judicial decisions," which Roosevelt espoused in a speech to the Ohio State Constitutional Convention in February 1912, further stamped him as a threat to the established order. His views on these constitutional issues were a large reason why his old friends, such as Root and Henry L. Stimson, decided to cast their lot with President Taft.

"I have absolutely no affiliations with any party."[81]

In the first two months of the campaign, Roosevelt struggled to get traction. Battles with La Follette supporters proved a continuing distraction. Meanwhile, President Taft amassed a wide lead in pledged convention delegates. To counter the impression of Taft as a shoo-in, Roosevelt and his aides challenged many of the delegates chosen in southern states. That tactic held down Taft's lead as reported in the press until Roosevelt could run in states where Republican voters chose delegates in open primaries. Since Roosevelt believed that the nomination ought to be his, he looked with increasing disgust at what he regarded as the dishonest tactics of his opponent. If the machinations of the Taft camp should cost him the Republican nomination, he wondered, would a third-party candidacy be something to consider?

The back-and-forth with Taft, which featured harsh language from both men, obscured the larger message that Roosevelt was offering. "This country will not be a good place for any of us to live in if it is not a reasonably good place for all of us to live in," he said in Louisville, Kentucky, on April 3, 1912.[82] That month his campaign caught fire, and he amassed primary wins in Illinois, Pennsylvania, Maine, and Oregon. It looked as if Roosevelt might sweep the nomination until Taft eked out a narrow victory in Massachusetts on April 30.

Roosevelt won further primary victories in May, but Taft remained in the lead in pledged or committed votes. With 1,078 delegates, 540 votes were needed to win in Chicago. On the eve of the convention, Roosevelt had 401 delegates, Taft had 201, minor candidates had 46, and 166 delegates were uninstructed but leaning toward Taft. Of the 254 delegates under challenge, most were in the Taft column. The result would come down to how the Republican National Committee dealt with these contested votes in the week before the convention met. Taft's control of that crucial panel resulted in the allocation of 235 delegates to the president and 19 to Roosevelt. Convinced that the nomination was being stolen from him and already thinking of a third-party candidacy, Roosevelt decided to break with precedent and attend the national convention in person.

When he arrived in Chicago, he told the assembled reporters that he felt "like a bull moose." For the candidate, who had hunted moose in the Maine woods in his youth, there was no more compelling image of natural vigor. Cartoonists soon began depicting Roosevelt as a moose, and the animal became a symbol first of Roosevelt's cause at the Republican convention and later of the his newly formed third party.[83]

Despite Roosevelt's presence, the convention remained in the control of the Taft forces. Facing disunity among the progressives arising from the opposition of La Follette, the Roosevelt delegates lost several test votes on procedural matters. Roosevelt concluded that the convention was rigged and, in effect, conceded the Republican nomination to Taft. Assured of the funds to run a third-party campaign, he bolted the convention and urged his delegates not to take part in any further proceedings. In a dramatic speech to his followers, he proclaimed, "We fight in honorable fashion for the good of mankind; fearless of the future; unheeding of our individual fates; with unflinching hearts and undimmed eyes; we stand at Armageddon and we battle for the Lord."[84]

"Our cause is based on the eternal principle of righteousness, and even though we who now lead may for the time fail, in the end the cause itself shall triumph."[85]

The Progressive Party, founded officially in August 1912, became Roosevelt's vehicle for his White House run. Once the Democrats had nominated Woodrow Wilson as their candidate in early July, Roosevelt's chances were slim in a three-cornered race against the Democrats and the Republicans. He understood the likelihood of his defeat, but he wanted to get across his reform ideas to the public. A presidential race would capitalize on his fame and allow him to reach more of his fellow citizens than any other way. In that sense, Roosevelt made the most of his historic opportunity.

In a speech to the Progressive Party convention in August 1912, the candidate laid out an agenda of substantive action that was far more reformist than that of any Democratic or Republican presidential nominees until the New Deal twenty years later. He wanted government regulation of large corporations through an industrial commission, a graduated inheritance tax on large fortunes, a "living wage" for all industrial workers, a minimum wage for women, a national department of health, and the creation of an insurance program for old age. In an election notable for the presence of women at all levels of the campaign among the Progressives and Democrats, Roosevelt's endorsement of woman suffrage and programs aimed at women stood out among the three major-party candidates. His positions gained him the endorsement of such reformers as Jane Addams and Florence Kelley. "I do not believe there is identity of function between men and women," he said in August 1912, "but I do believe there should be equality of right."[86]

Roosevelt proposed "to put at the service of all our people the collective power of the people, through their governmental agencies, alike in the nation and in the several States."[87] The Progressives fell short on the race issue because Roosevelt hoped to conciliate white reformers in the South by excluding black Republican converts from his third party. Otherwise, what was now called the Bull Moose Party looked to a more just society in ways that neither of the major parties was advancing. In fact, the national convention was as much a revival meeting as a political gathering. The assembled delegates sang to the tune of "Maryland, My Maryland":

Thou wilt not cower in the dust,
    Roosevelt, O Roosevelt!
Thy gleaming sword shall never rust,
    Roosevelt, O Roosevelt!
In thee we hail a leader just
In thee repose a sacred trust
To crush the powers of greed and lust,
    Roosevelt, O Roosevelt![88]

He did not label his program the New Nationalism, as he had done two years earlier, but his assertion of federal power and strong executive leadership put him in conflict with Woodrow Wilson's New Freedom creed. The two men conducted a long-distance debate about the future of progressivism during September and the first half of October 1912. Wilson warned of Roosevelt's zeal for power and emphasized competition in curbing corporate excesses. Roosevelt said that Wilson "is against using the power of the government to help the people to whom the government belongs." The attacks on Wilson that Roosevelt leveled failed to shake the lead that the Democratic nominee had established over the Republicans and the Progressives.[89]

A brush with death came when Roosevelt was shot in Milwaukee, Wisconsin, on October 14, 1912. A few minutes later, with the bullet still in his body, he told an amazed audience that "it takes more than that to kill a Bull Moose."[90] Popular sympathy flowed to Roosevelt, but the assassination attempt did not alter the political equation. When the votes were cast, Roosevelt came in second with eighty-eight electoral votes from six states. It was the best showing of any third party up to that time, and his electoral total has never since been exceeded by a third-party candidate. More important, the ideas he had put forward formed the unfinished agenda of first a major strand of progressivism and then the foundation of liberalism in the United States.

"I believe firmly that ninety per cent of the Republican Party would like to follow our lead or have a coalition with us on the basis of our platform. But I do not see how it is to be achieved under the present Republican leadership."[91]

Party building was not a task that Roosevelt relished, and the Progressives weakened without the immediate focus of a presidential election. A year after the election, Roosevelt embarked with his son Kermit on an expedition to explore the Amazon basin in Brazil. The hazardous journey brought Roosevelt to the brink of death, and he even contemplated staying behind to die while the others went on. He emerged from the ordeal in late April 1914; a reporter who saw him a month later observed: "He looks like hell. All kicked in, face drawn, utterance slow and weak, by comparison with what it was, and his walk awkward as the result of the injury" to his leg.[92] Roosevelt never regained the robust health he had displayed in the presidency. Meanwhile, the Progressive Party lagged in the 1914 off-year elections, and it was evident that Roosevelt had no genuine interest in his creation.

The outbreak of World War I in August 1914 changed the landscape and gave Roosevelt his last great political cause to pursue. He did not come out on the side of the Allied Powers against Imperial Germany at once, but by early 1915 he had concluded that the United States ought to intervene to prevent a German triumph. That position, while popular with some conservatives on the East Coast, conflicted with President Wilson's call for the nation to remain neutral between the warring sides. By this time, Roosevelt had come to have an intense dislike for the president, both as a man and a national leader. He poured out letters to friends with scornful references to how much he "cordially despised" Wilson and his government.[93] He advanced his public criticisms of Wilson in the *Metropolitan* magazine, which had replaced the *Outlook* as a major source of his writing income.

Roosevelt's continuing fascination for Americans was evident when a New York Republican, William A. Barnes Jr., sued the former president for libel. Roosevelt had called the conservative Barnes a political boss. The British ambassador and old friend of Roosevelt, Cecil Spring Rice, reported that his "great popularity is apparent in the way in which everybody is reading the reports of the trial now begun at Syracuse. Full telegraphic reports are being sent to all parts of the country and are read with great avidity. T.R. never bores the public." The jury found in favor of Roosevelt in May 1915. When an unwary friend asked him "how much damages" he had received, a smiling Roosevelt replied "My dear fel-low. *I* was the de-*fend*-ant."[94]

Keeping the public interested, however, placed a great strain on Roosevelt's personal affairs. Mail deluged his home and office at the rate of fifty thousand pieces per year. In 1918, he reported receiving four to five thousand letters a week. When he went out in public he still attracted a crowd. "I have found by practical experience that I can't go anywhere without it being universally advertised." Yet

Roosevelt encouraged press coverage of his activities and accommodated the newsmen who staked out his home at Oyster Bay. As one journalist wrote, "Watching T.R. at Sagamore Hill possessed some of the excitement of observing from a news out-post as close as possible to a volcano."[95]

"Every trouble we have at this moment in this country is primarily due to Wilson."[96]

As the controversy over World War I and American neutrality grew, Roosevelt identified more and more with the Allied cause. When the Germans torpedoed the British liner *Lusitania* in May 1915, he advocated intervention to punish Berlin for "piracy on a vaster scale of murder than old-time pirates ever practiced."[97] If Roosevelt were to become president again, the clear implication was that he would take the United States into the war against the German empire. Republicans feared that a Roosevelt candidacy might alienate the pro-neutrality public who comprised a majority of voters.

To have any political future, Roosevelt believed that he had to make a run at the GOP nomination, but his chances were marginal at best. Among conservatives, memories of his defection in 1912 were still fresh. He had met with Taft in public during 1915, but they showed no semblance of a reconciliation. More important, Roosevelt's candidacy was anathema to the large bloc of German American voters in key Midwestern states whom he had accused of divided loyalties. He knew that he could prevail only if "the country has in its mood something of the heroic."[98]

Instead of Roosevelt, the Republicans turned to Supreme Court justice and former New York governor Charles Evans Hughes. On the bench since 1910, Hughes was untainted by the battles of 1912 and seemed a compelling choice. Roosevelt abandoned what remained of the Progressive Party and came out, with some reluctance, for Hughes and the Republican ticket. He opposed Wilson, he said in print, "because his actions as a whole have been fraught with degradation and dishonor to this country, because he has dulled the moral sense of our people, and has weakened their power to do right, and because, unless we repudiate him at the polls, we, as a people, ourselves become responsible for the evil that he has done in our name."[99]

The narrow reelection of Wilson left the former president more disillusioned than ever with the state of American politics. When war came in April 1917 after the Germans announced unrestricted submarine warfare against the United States, Roosevelt felt vindicated and pledged his public support for the administration and the war effort. In private, he told one of his sons that "Wilson and his crowd should be in the Boche trenches."[100]

Roosevelt then announced his intention to take a division of the American army to France and attack the German fortifications himself. His campaign to raise a division in the spring of 1917 brought him into direct confrontation with the White House. For Roosevelt, his effort represented a patriotic commitment to American victory and a symbolic statement of the nation's support for the Allies. If his own life should be "lost" in the process, that would be a worthy sacrifice for a noble cause.

But there was a large element of self-delusion in his announcement. Roosevelt was fifty-nine, blind in one eye from an athletic accident while in the White House, wracked with illness, and devoid of substantial military experience in handling large bodies of troops. He would have to learn the art of commanding soldiers in trench warfare in a profession that now required stamina, patience, and insight into topography and enemy intentions. Moreover, the technology of warfare had changed since 1898. The Spanish had not deployed machine guns at Kettle Hill. Roosevelt intended to learn on the job, but his troops would have to pay the tuition for his instruction with their blood. At one point, Roosevelt told Elihu Root that if he went to France, he was not likely to return. Convince Wilson of that, Root quipped, and the president would let him go.

For the Wilson administration, which intended to assemble an army through conscription rather than volunteerism, Roosevelt's proposal seemed bizarre. Given Roosevelt's reluctance to submit to discipline when he played a subordinate role, it was hardly surprising that Wilson and the War Department rejected his offer. The snub further contributed to the hatred that the former president felt for the man in the White House. Roosevelt sent his four sons into battle, and continued to assail the administration and clamor for a more aggressive war policy.

"Please put out the light."[101]

During the last year of his life, Roosevelt returned to his Republican roots. He reconciled, at least in public, with Taft and Root, and spoke out for GOP candidates in the 1918 congressional elections. He supported the candidacy of Will H. Hays for chair of the Republican National Committee. President Wilson, Roosevelt contended, was guilty of "very grave faults and shortcomings and delays in governmental work." The Republicans represented "completely disinterested patriotism." There should be only "one language in this country—the English," he proclaimed. At the same, he reiterated the point he had made in 1912: "We can neither afford to be dogmatic individualists nor dogmatic in a blind belief in collectivism."[102]

With an eye on 1920, Republicans of all stripes were saying that Theodore Roosevelt would be the logical choice to lead the party in the next presidential contest. He still had the charisma that entranced the public. In January 1918, when he visited PS 40 in New York City to inspect a clinic for the undernourished, children poured out of their classrooms, shouting: "Roosevelt is here! Roosevelt is here! Roosevelt! Roosevelt!"[103]

A presidential run in 1920 was not to be. During the summer of 1918, Quentin Roosevelt, an aviator and the youngest of the four sons, was killed in a dogfight in France. The news stunned his mother and father, and Roosevelt's health declined. His wife later wrote that "the sorrows of the whole world bore heavily on Theodore the last months of his life."[104]

As the British and French gained ascendancy over the Germans on the Western Front in the fall of 1918, Wilson laid out the peace terms that would bring the fighting to a conclusion. Roosevelt and the Republicans pushed for a settlement that left no doubt about the defeat of Germany and her allies. The president's call for the election of a Democratic Congress to strengthen his bargaining position in making peace outraged Roosevelt, Henry Cabot Lodge, and most other Republicans. The former president wrote

letters to friends in England undercutting Wilson's negoti-
ating positions and emphasizing the president's political
weakness. For Roosevelt, politics did not end at the water's
edge in 1918; it went for a transatlantic cruise. It seems
probable that he would have joined the opponents of the
League of Nations in the battle that ensued in 1919.

Following his son's death, Roosevelt's health remained
poor as he exerted himself for the Republicans and the
war effort. During the fall of 1918, he spoke at bond
rallies and political events where "the very air seemed to
be alive with militant patriotism." Yet colleagues noted in
October "that he was not quite as fit as usual." A friend of
Henry Stimson likened Roosevelt to a volcano becoming
extinct. The literary critic Edmund Wilson recalled years
later seeing the "red faced and beefy ex-President" wearing
"the self-produced mask of the public man." After several
extended hospital stays, Roosevelt died at Oyster Bay on
the morning of January 6, 1919. His last words to his
valet, James Otis, were "Please put out the light."[105]

In 2010, a poll of "American Presidents: Greatest and
Worst," rated Theodore Roosevelt as the second-best
chief executive in American history, trailing only his distant cousin (and the husband of his niece Eleanor)
Franklin D. Roosevelt.[106] This lofty position attested to
the fascination that the Republican Roosevelt still inspires

in the minds of scholars and the public. It was not always so. In the three decades after his death, his reputation faded. After the Second World War, however, with the international challenges of the Cold War years, Roosevelt's vigorous assertion of the national interest and the realism of his foreign policy brought renewed attention to his life and times.

Roosevelt's life can be divided into three broad sections. His rise to the White House is a compelling drama as he surmounted every obstacle to achieve his ambition. His two terms in the White House were lively, although they lacked the crisis and danger that many of his twentieth- and twenty-first-century successors confronted. For his admirers, these were years of special achievements in world diplomacy.

Ironically, his most significant contribution came not while he held executive power but during Taft's presidency, with his decision to run as the Progressive Party candidate. Doomed to failure because of the structure of national politics, Roosevelt's third-party bid nevertheless succeeded in broadening the agenda of public life and inspiring other reformers. The ideological structure of American politics still reflects the priorities he advanced as the champion of the Bull Moose.

In his personal life, Roosevelt reflected the changes in culture that were bringing on modern ways of governing the nation. His personalization of the presidency, especially with his emphasis on family and his own vigorous lifestyle, began the infusion of entertainment techniques such as photo opportunities and staged events into the White House. As a former president, he capitalized on his celebrity status to sustain a political career. Much of his charisma derived from his ability to make the art of governance a compelling spectacle. There was a sense of fun about Roosevelt in power that still lingers amid the now dusty records of his career. When he died, a reporter observed, "You had to hate the Colonel a whole lot to keep from loving him."[107] While there were unlovely aspects in Roosevelt's life—his racial views, his abuses of power, his unfairness to opponents—there were also the very positive attributes he brought to politics in the control of corporations, commitment to conservation, and advocacy of progressive regulation. He believed in democratic government and practiced it with boundless energy. In an age when politics reeks with cynicism and selfish motives, the idealism of a Theodore Roosevelt would be as refreshing today as it was when he occupied the bully pulpit.

Notes

1. Kathleen Dalton, *Theodore Roosevelt: A Strenuous Life* (New York, 2002); Edmund Morris, *Colonel Roosevelt* (New York, 2010).

2. For examples of this genre, see David Reed, *The President's Weekend* (Poughkeepsie, NY, 2001); Matt Braun, *Dakota* (New York, 2005); Morton Kurland, *Theodore Roosevelt Rides Again* (Rancho Mirage, CA, 2006); and Terry Row, *Untarnished Reputation* (Santa Barbara, CA, 2009).

3. James M. Strock, *Theodore Roosevelt on Leadership: Executive Lessons from the Bully Pulpit* (New York, 2001); Daniel Ruddy, *Theodore Roosevelt's History of the United States: His Own Words, Selected and Arranged by Daniel Ruddy* (Washington, DC, 2010).

4. Ronald J. Pestritto, "Theodore Roosevelt Was No Conservative," *Wall Street Journal*, December 27, 2008.

5. Harry Thurston Peck, "President Roosevelt," *Bookman* 29 (March 1909): 26, 27.

6. Ibid., 27.

7. Corinne Roosevelt Robinson, *My Brother Theodore Roosevelt* (New York, 1921), 262.

8. John Dewey, "Theodore Roosevelt," *The Dial*, February 8, 1919, 115.

9. Lawrence F. Abbott, *Impressions of Theodore Roosevelt* (Garden City, NY, 1920), 267.

10. Theodore Roosevelt, *The Works of Theodore Roosevelt,* vol. 20, *Autobiography* (New York, 1926), 9. Hereinafter *Autobiography*.

11. Dalton, *Strenuous Life*, 68.

12. "Athletics, Scholarship, and Public Service," Address at the Harvard Union, February 23, 1907, in Theodore Roosevelt, *The Works of Theodore Roosevelt*, 20 vols. (New York, 1926), 13:564. Hereinafter *Works*.

13. David G. McCullough, *Mornings on Horseback* (New York, 1982), 162; *New York Tribune*, September 22, 1901.

14. Henry F. Pringle, *Theodore Roosevelt: A Biography* (New York, 1931), 33; Theodore Roosevelt to Anna Roosevelt, October 13, 1879, in *The Letters of Theodore Roosevelt*, ed. Elting E. Morison, 8 vols. (Cambridge, MA, 1951–54), 1:41, 42. Hereinafter *Letters*.

15. Carleton Putnam, *Theodore Roosevelt*, vol. 1, *The Formative Years,* 1858–1886 (New York, 1958), 168, 171.

16. *Autobiography*, 20:58.

17. "Conversation with Mr. Root at his apt. Nov. 3, 1934," Philip Jessup Papers, Library of Congress.

18. Theodore Roosevelt (hereinafter TR) to Theodore Roosevelt Jr., October 20, 1903, Theodore Roosevelt Papers, Library of Congress. Hereinafter Roosevelt Papers.

19. *Washington Evening Critic*, April 24, 1884.

20. Pringle, *Theodore Roosevelt*, 51.

21. William Henry Smith to Rutherford B. Hayes, June 9, 1884, Rutherford B. Hayes Papers, Rutherford B. Hayes Memorial Library, Fremont, Ohio.

22. "Theodore Roosevelt at Newark," *New-York Tribune*, October 25, 1884.

23. *Autobiography*, 98.

24. "Theodore Roosevelt: His Prompt Pursuit and Capture of Three Thieves in Dakota," *New York Times*, April 25, 1886.

25. James F. Vivian, ed., *The Romance of My Life: Theodore Roosevelt's Speeches in Dakota* (Fargo, ND, 1989), 60.

26. "Mr. Roosevelt Accepts," *New-York Tribune*, October 17, 1886.

27. Pringle, *Roosevelt*, 122.

28. TR to Anna Roosevelt, January 7, 1894, in *Letters*, 1:345.

29. Lincoln Steffens, *The Autobiography of Lincoln Steffens* (New York, 1931), 257.

30. Howard Lawrence Hurwitz, *Theodore Roosevelt and Labor in New York State, 1880–1900* (New York, 1943), 182.

31. TR to Henry White, April 30, 1897, Roosevelt Papers.

32. "Washington's Forgotten Maxim," *Works*, 13:185.

33. TR to George Dewey, February 25, 1898, in *Letters*, 1:784–85.

34. Pringle, *Roosevelt*, 195; *New York Tribune*, July 25, 1902.

35. William Henry Harbaugh, *Power and Responsibility: The Life and Times of Theodore Roosevelt* (New York, 1961), 111.

36. Pringle, *Roosevelt*, 214.

37. Frederick W. Holls to Albert Shaw, June 26, 1900, Albert Shaw Papers, New York Public Library.

38. TR to Cecil Spring Rice, November 19, 1900, *Letters*, 2:1424.

39. Marcus A. Hanna to William McKinley, June 25, 1900, William McKinley Papers, Library of Congress; emphasis in the original.

40. "Roosevelt and Presidency," *New-York Tribune*, August 1, 1901.

41. Roosevelt's statement is in "Theodore Roosevelt," *American Monthly Review of Reviews* 34 (October 1901): 438; Henry White to Henry Cabot Lodge, September 14, 1901, Henry Cabot Lodge Papers, Massachusetts Historical Society, Boston (second quotation); Louis T. Michener to Eugene Gano Hay, October 21, 1901, Eugene Gano Hay Papers, Library of Congress (last quotation).

42. TR to Lodge, September 23, 1901, Roosevelt Papers.

43. George H. Lyman to Lodge, November 13, 1901, Lodge Papers; Mark Sullivan, *Our Times: The United States 1900–1925*, vol. 3, *Pre-War America* (New York, 1930), 73.

44. Lyman Abbott, "A Review of President Roosevelt's Administration: IV—Its Influence on Patriotism and Public Service," *Outlook* 91, February 27, 1909, 430; Morley quoted in John Hay Diary, November 12, 1904, John Hay Papers, Library of Congress.

45. Owen Wister, *Roosevelt: The Story of a Friendship, 1880–1919* (New York, 1929), 87.

46. Day Allen Willey, "When You Meet the President," *Independent* 56 (June 30, 1904): 1487; William Allen White to Cyrus Leland, December 19, 1901, William Allen White Papers, Library of Congress.

47. Walter Clark to Erastus Brainerd, January 26, 1906, Erastus Brainerd Papers, University of Washington Library.

48. *Addresses and Presidential Messages of Theodore Roosevelt, 1902–1904* (New York, 1904), 9.

49. Ibid., 15.

50. *Autobiography*, 421.

51. *Addresses and Presidential Messages*, 121.

52. TR to Hay, August 19, 1903, Roosevelt Papers.

53. TR to George O. Trevelyan, May 28, 1904, Roosevelt Papers.

54. J. Hampton Moore to William Loeb, February 24, 1904, J. Hampton Moore Papers, Historical Society of Pennsylvania.

55. "Democratic Objections to Democratic Possibilities," *The Literary Digest* 28 (1904): 398.

56. Albert Shaw to W. T. Stead, October 7, 1904, Shaw Papers.

57. For Parker's charge, see *Washington Post*, Oct 24, 1904; *Washington Post*, November 5, 1904, carried Roosevelt's pledge.

58. *New York Tribune*, November 9, 1904.

59. TR to Joseph B. Bishop, March 27, 1905, *Letters*, 4:1145.

60. TR to Kermit Roosevelt, June 13, 1906, Roosevelt Papers.

61. TR to Lyman Abbott, July 1, 1906, Roosevelt Papers.

62. *Autobiography*, 544.

63. TR to William Howard Taft, August 21, 1907, *Letters*, 5:762.

64. *State Papers*, 257.

65. *Autobiography*, 386.

66. TR to Taft, August 7, 1908, *Letters*, 6:1157.

67. TR to George O. Trevelyan, June 19, 1908, *Letters*, 6:1085.

68. William Howard Taft to TR, November 7, 1908, William Howard Taft Papers, Library of Congress.

69. Lucius B. Swift to Mrs. Swift, July 8, 1910, Lucius B. Swift Papers, Indiana State Library, Indianapolis.

70. TR to Theodore Roosevelt Jr., January 31, 1909, *Letters*, 6:1499; "A Short Measure of What President Roosevelt Has Done," *World's Work* 17 (March 1909): 11314.

71. Joseph L. Bristow to J. R. Harrison, February 4, 1909, Joseph L. Bristow Papers, Kansas State Historical Society.

72. Elihu Root to Whitelaw Reid, Dec 20, 1909, Whitelaw Reid Papers, Library of Congress.

73. TR to Whitelaw Reid, May 2, 1910, *Letters*, 7:78.

74. Alexander Walker, *Stardom: The Hollywood Phenomenon* (London, 1974), 13.

75. Daniel Boorstin, *The Image, or What Happened to the American Dream* (New York, 1962), 57.

76. John Callan O'Laughlin, *From the Jungle through Europe with Roosevelt* (Boston, 1910), 115.

77. TR to Henry Cabot Lodge, May 5, 1910, *Letters*, 7:80.

78. Theodore Roosevelt, *The New Nationalism* (New York, 1910), 5, 11–12, 28.

79. TR to Arthur Lee, May 10, 1912, Papers of Lord Lee of Fareham, Courtauld Institute, London.

80. Conversation with Mr. Root at 998 Fifth Avenue, December 7, 1931, Philip Jessup Papers; *New York Times*, February 23, 1912.

81. TR to James Bronson Reynolds, June 11, 1912, *Letters*, 7:561.

82. *Works*, 17:188.

83. John A. Gable, *The Bull Moose Years: Theodore Roosevelt and the Progressive Party* (Port Washington, NY, 1978), 19.

84. *Works*, 17:231.

85. Ibid., 298.

86. Lewis L. Gould, ed., *Bull Moose on the Stump: The 1912 Campaign Speeches of Theodore Roosevelt* (Lawrence, KS, 2008), 51.

87. Ibid., 254.

88. "Songs to be Sung at the First National Progressive Convention," August 1912 (Chicago, 1912).

89. *Works*, 17:314.

90. Gould, *Bull Moose*, 175.

91. TR to Lemuel Quigg, May 20, 1913, Roosevelt Papers.

92. Ashmun Brown to Erastus Brainerd, May 28, 1914, Brainerd Papers.

93. TR to Meyer Lissner, November 16, 1914, *Letters*, 8:845.

94. Charles Willis Thompson, *Presidents I've Known and Two Near Presidents* (Indianapolis, 1929), 114–15; Lewis L. Gould, "The Price of Fame: Theodore Roosevelt as a Celebrity, 1909–1919," *Lamar Journal of the Humanities* 10 (1984): 9.

95. Roosevelt to Gustavus Pope, March 2, 1915, Roosevelt Papers; Julian Street, "On the Jump with Roosevelt, *Collier's*, June 10, 1916, 6.

96. TR to Arthur Lee, March 17, 1917, Lee Papers.

97. Harbaugh, *Power and Responsibility*, 476.

98. *Letters*, 8:1024.

99. "Wilson Broke Faith, Says T. R.," *New York Tribune*, November 1, 1916.

100. TR to Kermit Roosevelt, June 8, 1917, Kermit Roosevelt Papers, Library of Congress.

101. Pringle, *Roosevelt*, 602.

102. "Roosevelt Calls War Mismanaged," *New York Times*, March 29, 1918.

103. Henry Dwight Chapin, "A Little Journey with Theodore Roosevelt," *Outlook*, October 22, 1924, 286.

104. Edith Kermit Roosevelt to Arthur Lee, March 5, 1920, Lee Papers.

105. "Roosevelt Attacks Wilson's Appeal," *New York Tribune*, October 29, 1918; Ralph Stout, ed., *Roosevelt in the Kansas City Star* (Boston, 1921), xliii; Edmund Wilson, *The Bit between My Teeth* (New York, 1965), 76; Henry L. Stimson, "My Last Three Interviews with Theodore Roosevelt," Henry L. Stimson Papers, Yale University.

106. Siena Research Institute, "American Presidents: Greatest and Worst," news release, July 1, 2010, available at www.siena.edu/uploadedfiles/home/parents_and_community/community_page/sri/independent_research/Presidents%20Release_2010_final.pdf .

107. Harbaugh, *Power and Responsibility*, 520.

Bibliography

The main collection of Theodore Roosevelt Papers is housed at the Library of Congress and has been available on microfilm since 1969. A project at Dickinson State University's Theodore Roosevelt Center in North Dakota (www.theodorerooseveltcenter.org), is digitizing all the Roosevelt letters and documents that can be found. When this endeavor is completed, Roosevelt's correspondence will be online for anyone to consult and use. Roosevelt wrote or dictated an estimated hundred thousand letters during his life. Some ten thousand of them were published in Elting E. Morison et al., eds., *The Letters of Theodore Roosevelt*, 8 vols. (Cambridge, MA, 1951–54), and these volumes are the most convenient way to find the essential Roosevelt. For Roosevelt's published writings, see *The Works of Theodore Roosevelt*, 20 vols. (New York, 1926). Lewis L. Gould, ed., *Bull Moose on the Stump: The 1912 Campaign Speeches of*

Theodore Roosevelt (Lawrence, KS, 2008), documents Roosevelt's most exciting presidential race.

The major biographical treatments of Roosevelt began with Henry F. Pringle, *Theodore Roosevelt: A Biography* (New York, 1931), which treats him as an individual who never grew up. John Morton Blum, *The Republican Roosevelt* (Cambridge, MA, 1954) offers an influential interpretation of Roosevelt as a strong, effective president. Carleton Putnam, *Theodore Roosevelt*, vol. 1, *The Formative Years, 1858–1886* (New York, 1958) is the only published volume of what was intended to be a longer treatment of Roosevelt's life. William H. Harbaugh, *Power and Responsibility: The Life and Times of Theodore Roosevelt* (New York, 1961), was the standard one-volume study for almost half a century.

A major multivolume project on Roosevelt is Edmund Morris, *The Rise of Theodore Roosevelt* (New York, 1979), *Theodore Rex* (New York, 2001), and *Colonel Roosevelt* (New York, 2010). Lewis L. Gould, *The Presidency of Theodore Roosevelt* (Lawrence, KS, 1991, 2nd ed. 2011) considers Roosevelt's record in office. David G. McCullough, *Mornings on Horseback* (New York, 1982), offers a well-documented and engagingly written treatment of Roosevelt from youth to early manhood. John Milton Cooper Jr., *The Warrior and the Priest: Woodrow Wilson and Theodore Roosevelt* (Cambridge, MA, 1983) contrasts the lives of Roosevelt and Woodrow Wilson in a very graceful and influential book. H. W. Brands, *T. R.: The Last Romantic* (New York, 1997) surveys Roosevelt's psyche as it affected his political career. Kathleen Dalton, *Theodore*

Roosevelt: A Strenuous Life (New York, 2002) examines Roosevelt's personal and public life in rich detail and with a keen sense of the currents of historical interpretation. Douglas Brinkley, *The Wilderness Warrior: Theodore Roosevelt and the Crusade for America* (New York, 2009) delves into Roosevelt's conservation record up to 1909. Louis Auchincloss, *Theodore Roosevelt* (New York, 2001) and Aïda Donald, *Lion in the White House: A Life of Theodore Roosevelt* (New York, 2007) are shorter treatments of Roosevelt's life.

For specific phases of Roosevelt's career and his relations with his family, see George E. Mowry, *Theodore Roosevelt and the Progressive Movement* (Madison, WI, 1946); Howard K. Beale, *Theodore Roosevelt and the Rise of America to World Power* (Baltimore, MD, 1956); John A. Gable, *The Bull Moose Years: Theodore Roosevelt and the Progressive Party* (Port Washington, NY, 1978); Sylvia Jukes Morris, *Edith Kermit Roosevelt: Portrait of a First Lady* (New York, 1980); William N. Tilchin, *Theodore Roosevelt and the British Empire: A Study in Presidential Statecraft* (New York, 1997); Betty Boyd Caroli, *The Roosevelt Women* (New York, 1998); Stacy Cordery, *Theodore Roosevelt: In the Vanguard of the Modern* (Belmont, CA, 2003); Sarah Watts, *Rough Rider in the White House: Theodore Roosevelt and the Politics of Desire* (Chicago, 2003); Patricia O'Toole, *When Trumpets Call: Theodore Roosevelt After the White House* (New York, 2005); Stacy A. Cordery, *Alice: Alice Roosevelt Longworth, from White House Princess to Washington Power Broker* (New York, 2007); Paul M. Rego,

American Ideal: Theodore Roosevelt's Search for American Individualism (Lanham, MD, 2008); Joshua David Hawley, *Theodore Roosevelt; Preacher of Righteousness* (New Haven, CT, 2008); Sidney Milkis, *Theodore Roosevelt, the Progressive Party, and the Transformation of American Democracy* (Lawrence, KS, 2009); Serge Ricard, ed., *A Companion to Theodore Roosevelt* (Malden, MA, 2011); and Roger L. Di Silverstro, *Theodore Roosevelt in the Badlands: A Young Politician's Quest for Recovery in the American West* (New York, 2011).

The Theodore Roosevelt Association (www.theodoreroosevelt .org) publishes the *Theodore Roosevelt Association Journal*, which tracks the latest scholarship on his life and times.